Behold the Lamb

A Scripture-based, Modern, Messianic
Pesach Memorial 'Avodah

Compiled by Kevin Geoffrey

PERFECT *Word*
P · U · B · L · I · S · H · I · N · G

A ministry of Perfect Word Ministries

⁓⌣ ⌣⌣⌐

You are encouraged to prepare your heart for the
'avodah by reading "It Is a Sacrifice" from the **Messianic
Mo'adiym Devotional**, available from Perfect Word.

⌐⌣⌢ ⌢⌣⌐

Hebrew on Front Cover: הנה השה, *Hineh HaSeh*—"Behold the Lamb"

Scripture quotations are indicated by italics.

The Name יהוה is represented by the name "ADONAI" in capital letters.
The title אֱלֹהִים is represented by "GOD" in capital letters.

PERFECT *Word*
P · U · B · L · I · S · H · I · N · G
A ministry of Perfect Word Ministries

PO BOX 82954 Phoenix, AZ 85071
www.PerfectWordMinistries.org
1-888-321-PWMI

ISBN #: 0-9785504-7-1

Printed in the United States of America

All Scriptures taken from *Young's Literal Translation of the Holy Bible*
(1862/1898), with the names "Jesus" and "Christ" rendered "Yeshua" and
"Messiah," respectively. Archaic English words such as "thee" and "thou" have
been updated. Where deemed appropriate, other words and phrases were re-
rendered using the original texts. Our updating for the modern Messianic
reader is ©2010 by Perfect Word Ministries, Inc.

Contents

Preface iii

Pesach Memorial 'Avodah 1

Changing the Way We "Do" Passover 31

   ॐ With Respect to Tradition 33

   ॐ Unraveling the Mystery of Matzah 35

   ॐ Keeping Vigil—A Lost Command 37

   ॐ Removing the Leaven 39

   ॐ Notes 41

Matzah Recipes 45

Children's Craft 49

Suggestions for the Facilitator 52

To Isaac, Josiah & Hosea

and all the sons of Israel

For *your* sons,
when they ask.

Preface

I GREW UP KEEPING PASSOVER as one of the few holidays that my family observed. Every Spring, out came the fancy china, the matzah ball soup, the brisket, the gefilte fish, the charoset, the afikomen, the bar mitzvah yarmulkes, Elijah's chair, the seder plate and its elements, and, of course, the Haggadah. My grandparents and aunt and uncle from across town would be there, and usually my other grandparents, great aunt, and aunt from Brooklyn would drive in as well. I remember that during these family get-togethers our home was always very loud with activity, which carried over into the seder. My dad would lead the seder, anxious to get to the *bo-re p'riy hagafen*, and my little sister would read the four questions—an honor coveted by her big brother. Of course, the "telling" was punctuated with my mother silently, but noticeably excusing herself to check on the progress of the food. This would begin a small exodus from the table consisting of my Aunt Mady and Grandma Berger.

Since the days of my youth, I have attended many different seders, both in homes and large groups. Some time after I became a believer in Yeshua, I learned of the *Messianic Passover Haggadah* from Lederer Publications, and Passover finally began to have meaning for me. My heritage as a Jew became reinforced in a way that had not happened during my youth. Needless to say, I greatly appreciated the *Messianic Passover Haggadah*, and rejoice in the many others that Messianic Jews all over the world continue to develop to this day.

As time went on, I began to study the Scriptures and the sources of various Jewish traditions. I eventually realized that while the core of the modern Passover seder is the telling of the story of the Exodus, many of the elements of the traditional seder are simply creative innovations not found in Scripture. I also came to realize that the *Pesach* was not the seder itself, but the actual animal that was to be sacrificed and eaten at the end of the fourteenth day of the first month. Through this process, I began to view the modern Jewish seder as it was originally intended—as a memorial. Like many Jewish traditions, the seder was created as a *substitute* to make up for the nation's current status in dispersion. Our modern minds have made it *the* Pesach, but I believe this misses the mark.

Behold the Lamb—A Scripture-based, Modern, Messianic Pesach Memorial 'Avodah ('avodah in this context means "service" or "rite" or "ceremony") is not intended to be a replacement for the Passover seder. Our 'Avodah is simply one *alternative* to the seder—it is another *substitute* for the *Pesach* we are unable to literally keep at this time. The Jewish seder contains a myriad of traditions that our people have observed for many years. In contrast, as you read our 'Avodah, you will notice the significant *absence* of the seder plate and other time-honored traditions associated with *Pesach*. Only three familiar elements make their appearance in our 'Avodah—the matzah, the maror, and the fruit of the vine—and these because we see them in the Scriptures.

The primary feature of the *Behold the Lamb Avodah* is that approximately 90% of the words on the page are direct quotes from Scripture (indicated by *italics*). The goal in creating this 'Avodah was simple: to produce a Scripture-based service that would help us to memorialize the *Pesach*. There was little attempt to make the service more lively, more entertaining, more meaningful, more Jewish, more Messianic, or anything else. We wanted to see what would happen if we let Scripture speak for itself—if we let Scripture tell the story, rather than trying to put it into our own words.

I pray that *Behold the Lamb* will help to deepen *and simplify* your *Pesach* memorial this year. May ADONAI richly bless you as you walk joyfully through this season of freedom!

In Yeshua,

Kevin Geoffrey

Pesach Memorial 'Avodah

*This service is intended to start at the very
beginning of sunset ending the fourteenth day of
the first month, according to the Scriptures.*

What Is This 'Avodah You Have?

FACILITATOR   And ADONAI spoke to מֹשֶׁה, Moshe, saying... "In the first month, on the fourteenth of the month, between the evenings [at twilight], is the פֶּסַח, Pesach to ADONAI." וַיִּקְרָא Leviticus 23:1 & 5 "You are to observe this thing, for [it is] a statute to you and to your sons—to the age. And it will be, when you come in to the land which ADONAI gives to you, as He has spoken, that you keep this עֲבֹדָה, 'avodah (service)." שְׁמוֹת Exodus 12:24-25

As the sun begins to set, closing this fourteenth day of the first month, let us prepare our hearts for ADONAI's appointed time. It is a time to remember how ADONAI delivered and redeemed His people—a time to remember ADONAI's provision and salvation.

As we recall the story of Pesach, we remember our beginnings as ADONAI's chosen people. We are reminded that we have been set apart from all the nations of the earth to uniquely serve ADONAI our God.

But the story of Pesach does not just serve to remind us of our beginnings. It helps us remember our very purpose on the earth: to declare the wondrous works of ADONAI, the God of יִשְׂרָאֵל, Yis'rael—that all the earth may know that He alone is God and there is none like Him.

The story of Pesach is the story of the rebirth of our people, a rebirth to which the Scriptures constantly urge us to return. And nowhere—and in no one— do we find that return more clearly than in our Messiah, Yeshua. He *is* our Pesach—our deliverer, our redeemer... our salvation.

Let us now begin the Pesach עֲבֹדָה, *'avodah.*

⁓⁓⁓⁓

SON   Abba, *what is this* עֲבֹדָה, *'avodah you have?* שְׁמוֹת Exodus 12:26

ABBA   It is *a sacrifice of Pesach to* ADONAI, *who passed over the houses of the sons of Yis'rael in Egypt when He struck down the Egyptians, and our houses He delivered.* שְׁמוֹת Exodus 12:27

SON   Abba, why are we to *take of the blood, and put it on the two side-posts and on the lintel over the houses in which we eat it?* שְׁמוֹת Exodus 12:7

ABBA   It is to remember that *the blood has become as a sign for us*—that when ADONAI saw *the blood, He passed over us, and a plague for destruction was not on us when He struck the land of Egypt.* שְׁמוֹת Exodus 12:13

SON   Abba, why do we *eat the meat... roasted with fire?* שְׁמוֹת Exodus 12:8

ABBA   ADONAI commanded us to not *eat it raw, or boiled at all in water, but roasted with fire,* so that *none of it may be left till morning.* שְׁמוֹת Exodus 12:9-10 In this, we remember how ADONAI's Pesach was *eaten in haste*—our *loins girded,* our *sandals on* our *feet, and* our *staffs in* our *hands.* שְׁמוֹת Exodus 12:11

SON   Abba, why do we eat the Pesach with מַצָּה, *matzah* (unleavened bread)?

ABBA	We eat the *matzah* to remember how the sons of Yis'rael *baked* עֻגֹת מַצּוֹת, *ugot matzot* (disks of matzah) *with the dough which they had brought out from Egypt. The dough had no* חָמֵץ, *chametz* (yeast), *for [the sons of Yis'rael] had been cast out of Egypt, and had not been able to delay or make provision for themselves.* שְׁמוֹת Exodus 12:39 *It is the bread of affliction; for in haste we came out of the land of Egypt. By eating the matzah, we will remember the day of our coming out of the land of Egypt all the days of our life.* דְּבָרִים Deuteronomy 16:3
SON	And why do we eat it with מָרֹר, *maror* (bitter herbs)?
ABBA	I do not know, my son—I only know that ADONAI commanded us to eat the Pesach with *maror*. Still, we will use it when we tell the story!
SON	Abba, I have one more question.
ABBA	Yes, my son?
SON	Abba, where is the Pesach? It is not here!
ABBA	My son, ADONAI tells us we may only *sacrifice the Pesach... at the place where* ADONAI *our* GOD *chooses to cause His name to tabernacle—in the land which* ADONAI *has given to us.* דְּבָרִים Deuteronomy 16:5-6 and שְׁמוֹת Exodus 12:25 Today, *the whole assembly of the congregation of Yis'rael is dispersed among the nations because we have been far from the ways of* ADONAI. שְׁמוֹת Exodus 12:6

But there is good news, because *our Pesach was sacrificed for us—Messiah!* 1Corinthians 5:7 So, though we may only observe the עֲבֹדָה, *'avodah* in part, still, *we may keep the feast!* 1Corinthians 5:8 For ADONAI is faithful to preserve us and cause His people to return to His ways. Indeed, this is what the story of Pesach is all about. |

Av'raham Aviynu

Our Father Av'raham

The story of Pesach begins with our father, אַבְרָהָם, Av'raham, once named אַבְרָם, Av'ram. Av'ram was called by ADONAI who said to him, "Go for your-self, from your land, your kindred, and from the house of your father, to the land which I will show you. And I [will] make you become a great nation, and bless you, and make your name great; and you [will] be a blessing. And I [will] bless those blessing you, and him who treats you as contemptible I [will] curse—and blessed in you will be all families of the earth."
בְּרֵאשִׁית Genesis 12:1-3

ADONAI made a covenant with Av'ram, saying, "To your seed I have given this land, from the river of Egypt to the great river, the river פְּרָת, P'rat." בְּרֵאשִׁית Genesis 15:18 And He said to Av'ram, "...know that your seed will be a sojourner in a land not theirs, and they will serve [the people of that land, who will] afflict them four hundred years. And the nation whom they [will] serve, I [will] also judge, and after this they [will] come out with great wealth."
בְּרֵאשִׁית Genesis 15:13-14

So it was that ADONAI gave to Av'ram a son, יִצְחָק, Yitz'chak, and to him a son, יַעֲקֹב, Ya'akov, who dwelled in the land of his father's sojournings—in the land of כְּנַעַן, K'na-an. בְּרֵאשִׁית Genesis 37:1

Then ADONAI gave to Ya'akov a son, יוֹסֵף, Yosef, whom Ya'akov loved... more than any of Yosef's brothers. The brothers saw this and they hated Yosef, and were not able to speak to him peaceably. בְּרֵאשִׁית Genesis 37:4

Then the brothers, having been moved with jealousy, conspired against Yosef and sold him to Egypt. But

God was with him, and delivered him out of all his tribulations. God gave Yosef favor and wisdom before Pharaoh king of Egypt, and he appointed him governor over Egypt and all his house. Acts 7:9-10 For what Yosef's brothers had devised against him for evil—GOD devised it for good. בְּרֵאשִׁית Genesis 50:20

A great famine soon came upon all the land of Egypt and K'na-an—great tribulation—and our fathers could not find sustenance. Then Ya'akov, having heard that there was grain in Egypt, sent forth our fathers... and Yosef made himself known to them.... Then Yosef sent and called for his father Ya'akov, and all his family, and they all came to live in Egypt in the land of Goshen. Acts 7:11-14 Thus, GOD sent Yosef ahead of Yis'rael to preserve a remnant in the land for them, and to give life to them by a great escape. בְּרֵאשִׁית Genesis 45:7

Yosef died, as did all his brothers and all that generation. But the sons of Yis'rael were fruitful, and they teemed and multiplied and were very, very mighty—the land was filled with them. שְׁמוֹת Exodus 1:6-7

Let us raise our cup and drink, and rejoice in the salvation of ADONAI!

ALL I have made you exceedingly fruitful... and I have established My covenant between Me and you, and your seed after you, to their generations, for an everlasting covenant... בְּרֵאשִׁית Genesis 17:6-7

ברוך אתה יי אלהינו מלך העולם בורא פרי הגפן

Baruch atah ADONAI 'eloheinu melech haolam bo-re p'riy hagafen

Blessed are you, ADONAI our God, King of the Universe, who creates the fruit of the vine.

ALL DRINK JOYFULLY, REFILL CUPS AS NEEDED.

A New King Arose

FACILITATOR But there arose a new king over Egypt, who did not know Yosef. And [the king] said to his people, "Behold, the people of the sons of Yis'rael are more numerous and mighty than we. Come, let us act wisely concerning them, lest they multiply, and it comes to pass that when war happens, they join our enemies and fight against us and go up out of the land." שְׁמוֹת Exodus 1:8-10

READER 1 So they set over Yis'rael taskmasters, so as to afflict them with forced labor. And they built store-cities for Pharaoh, Pithom and Raamses. But as they were afflicted, so did they multiply and spread out, and [the Egyptians] were full of loathing because of the sons of Yis'rael. שְׁמוֹת Exodus 1:11-12

READER 2 So the Egyptians forced the sons of Yis'rael to labor with cruelty, and made their lives bitter in hard service, in clay, and in brick, and in every kind of service in the field. All their service in which they labored was with cruelty. שְׁמוֹת Exodus 1:14

READER 3 Then Pharaoh laid a charge on all his people, saying, "Every [Hebrew] son who is born—into the River you must cast him... he must go into the River, that you may put him to death." שְׁמוֹת Exodus 1:22 & 16

FACILITATOR In all these ways, the people of Yis'rael were oppressed by Pharaoh and despised in the land of Egypt. To aid us in our memory, let us now taste of the maror, allowing it to remind us of the bitter slavery of our people.

ALL We labored with cruelty and suffered the death of our children.

**ALL TASTE THE MAROR
AND REFRAIN FROM DRINKING, IF POSSIBLE.**

Their Cry Went Up

FACILITATOR   And it came to pass that a son of Hebrew slaves, *Moshe, was born and was hidden for three months by his parents, because they saw that the child was beautiful, and they were not afraid of the decree of the king.* עִבְרִים Hebrews 11:23 Then he was placed in a basket upon the river, and *the daughter of Pharaoh found him and took him up, and reared him as her own son. And Moshe was taught in all wisdom of the Egyptians, and was powerful in words and in works.* Acts 7:21-22 *...having become great, Moshe eventually refused to be called a son of the daughter of Pharaoh, and by faith he left Egypt behind...* עִבְרִים Hebrews 11:24 & 27

During the long period that followed, the sons of Yis'rael groaned [with grief] because of the service [of slavery]. They cried [out], and their cry went up to GOD, because of their service [of slavery]. שְׁמוֹת Exodus 2:23

ALL   *And GOD heard their groaning, and He remembered His covenant with Av'raham, with Yitz'chak, and with Ya'akov.* שְׁמוֹת Exodus 2:24

FACILITATOR   One day, *Moshe came to the mountain of GOD... and there appeared to him a Messenger of ADONAI in a flame of fire out of the midst of a bush... a bush burning with fire, but not consumed.* שְׁמוֹת Exodus 3:1-2

ADONAI spoke to Moshe and said, "אֶהְיֶה אֲשֶׁר אֶהְיֶה, *eh'yeh 'asher eh'yeh... I am ADONAI, the GOD of your father, GOD of Av'raham, GOD of Yitz'chak, and GOD of Ya'akov.... This is My name, to the age; and this My memorial, to generation [after] generation.... I have certainly seen the affliction of My people who are in Egypt, and their cry—because of their oppressors—*

I have heard. I know their pain." שְׁמוֹת Exodus 3:14a, 15 & 6-7
Then ADONAI said:

ALL   *"I will go down to deliver Yis'rael out of the hand of the Egyptians, and to cause her to go up out of the land, into a land good and broad, into a land flowing with milk and honey..."* שְׁמוֹת Exodus 3:8

FACILITATOR   So ADONAI *sent Moshe to Pharaoh to bring His people, the sons of Yis'rael, out of Egypt.* שְׁמוֹת Exodus 3:10 ADONAI *said to Moshe, "In your going to turn back to Egypt, see— all the wonders which I have put in your hand—that [when] you have done them before Pharaoh, and I—I harden his heart, he will not let the people go."* שְׁמוֹת Exodus 4:21 Thus, Moshe went in to Pharaoh and said, "This is what ADONAI, GOD of Yis'rael, says, 'Let My people go, so they [may] keep a feast to Me in the wilderness.'" שְׁמוֹת Exodus 5:1

READER 1   *"Who is* ADONAI," *said Pharaoh, "that I [should] listen to His voice, to let Yis'rael go? I have not known* ADONAI, so *Yis'rael also I will not let go.... Lazy! You are lazy! That is why you say, 'Let us go, let us sacrifice to* ADONAI.'"

שְׁמוֹת Exodus 5:2 & 17

READER 2   *So Pharaoh commanded the oppressors among the people... saying, "Do not give anymore straw to the people for the making of bricks, as before—they* can go and gather straw for themselves. *However, the proper quantity of the bricks which you* previously put on them to make—*do not diminish from it..."* שְׁמוֹת Exodus 5:6-8

READER 3   The officials of the sons of Yis'rael met with Moshe and said to him, "May ADONAI *look upon you, and judge, because you have caused our fragrance to stink in the eyes of Pharaoh and in the eyes of his servants—to give a sword into their hand to slay us.... Straw is not given to* the people, and our taskmasters keep saying to us, *'Make bricks!' And behold, the people are being beaten...."* שְׁמוֹת Exodus 5:21 & 16

READER 4   *And Moshe turned back to* ADONAI *and said, "Lord, why have You done evil to this people? Why is this?... Since I have come to Pharaoh to speak in Your name, he has done evil to this people, and You have not delivered Your people at all!"* שְׁמוֹת Exodus 5:22-23

FACILITATOR   And so, Pharaoh began to tighten his fist around the sons of Yis'rael. Let us again taste of the *maror*, this time more liberally, and allow the bitter sting to remind us how the path to deliverance is often plagued with hardship and pain.

ALL   We met with greater punishment for seeking our freedom—we blamed our deliverer.

EAT LIBERALLY OF THE **MAROR**
AND REFRAIN FROM DRINKING, IF POSSIBLE.

The Ten Plagues

FACILITATOR   And ADONAI said to Moshe, "You—*speak all that I command you... and* Pharaoh *will let the sons of Yis'rael go out of his land. I will harden the heart of* Pharaoh, *and multiply My signs and My wonders in the land of Egypt. The Egyptians will know that I am ADONAI, in My stretching out My hand against Egypt; and I will bring out the sons of Yis'rael from their midst."*

שְׁמוֹת Exodus 7:2-3 & 5

The Plague of Blood

READER 1   *"Go to Pharaoh in the morning," said ADONAI, "and with your rod in your hand, say to him, 'ADONAI, GOD of the Hebrews, has sent me to you, saying, "Let My people go!... By this you will know that I am ADONAI: behold, I will strike with the rod which is in My hand, on the waters which are in the River, and they will be turned to blood—the fish that are in the River will die, and the River will stink, and the Egyptians will be wearied of drinking waters from the River."'"*

שְׁמוֹת Exodus 7:15-18

ALL   And it was so—the first plague. ADONAI struck Egypt with blood.

READER 1   *But the magicians of Egypt did the same with their secret arts, and the heart of Pharaoh was hardened— he did not listen to Moshe, as ADONAI had spoken. And Pharaoh turned and went in into his house, and did not concern his heart with it.* שְׁמוֹת Exodus 7:22-23

The Plague of Frogs

READER 2   *And ADONAI said to Moshe, "Go in to Pharaoh and say to him, 'This is what ADONAI says, "Let My people go!—*

that they [may] serve me. If you refuse to let [them] go, I will strike all your borders with frogs; and the River will teem with frogs, and they will go up and into your house, and into the inner-chamber of your bed, and on your couch, and into the house of your servants, and among your people, and into your ovens and your knead-ing-troughs. Yes, on you and on your people, and on all your servants will the frogs go up."" שְׁמוֹת Exodus 8:1-4

ALL   And it was so—the second plague. ADONAI struck Egypt with frogs.

READER 2   *And Pharaoh called for Moshe...and said,"Pray to ADONAI, that he turn aside the frogs from me and from my people, and I will let the people go, so they [can] sacrifice to ADONAI."* Moshe replied, *"According to your word* it will be done, *so that you will know that there is none like ADONAI our GOD."* שְׁמוֹת Exodus 8:8 & 10

ALL   *But when Pharaoh saw that there had been relief* from the plague of frogs, *he hardened his heart, and did not listen to* Moshe, *as ADONAI had spoken.* שְׁמוֹת Exodus 8:15

The Plague of Gnats

READER 3   *So ADONAI said to Moshe... "Stretch out your rod, and strike the dust of the land, and it will become gnats in all the land of Egypt."* Suddenly there were *gnats on man and beast—all the dust of the land became gnats in all the land of Egypt.* שְׁמוֹת Exodus 8:16-17

ALL   And it was so—the third plague. ADONAI struck Egypt with gnats.

READER 3   *The magicians tried to do the same with their secret arts, but they were unable... and the magicians said to Pharaoh, "It is the finger of GOD." But the heart of Phar-aoh was hard, and he did not listen to them, as ADONAI had spoken.* שְׁמוֹת Exodus 8:18-19

The Plague of Swarms

READER 4   Then ADONAI said to Moshe, "Say to Pharaoh, 'This is what ADONAI says, "Let My people go—[that] they [may] serve Me. If you do not let My people go, I will send against you, your servants, your people, and your houses, and also the ground on which they are, swarms [of insects]. And I will set apart in that day the land of גֹּשֶׁן, Goshen, in which My people are staying, that the swarms will not be there, so that you will know that I am ADONAI."'" שְׁמוֹת Exodus 8:20-22

ALL   And it was so—the fourth plague. ADONAI struck Egypt with swarms.

READER 4   And Pharaoh called to Moshe... and said, "I will let you go and you can sacrifice to ADONAI your GOD in the wilderness, only do not go very far off. Pray for me." Moshe replied, "I will go out from you and pray to ADONAI, and the swarm will turn aside from you... only do not let Pharaoh deceive again in not letting the people go to sacrifice to ADONAI." שְׁמוֹת Exodus 8:28-29

ALL   But Pharaoh hardened his heart again... and did not let the people go. שְׁמוֹת Exodus 8:32

The Plague of Cattle Disease

READER 5   And ADONAI said to Moshe, "Go in to Pharaoh and say to him, 'This is what ADONAI, GOD of the Hebrews, says, "Let My people go, [that] they [may] serve Me, for if you refuse to let [them] go and continue holding onto them, the hand of ADONAI will be on your cattle... a grievous pestilence will be on them...."'" שְׁמוֹת Exodus 9:1-4

ALL   And it was so—the fifth plague. ADONAI struck Egypt with cattle disease.

READER 5   ADONAI did this thing the next day, and all the cattle of Egypt died, but of the cattle of the sons of Yis'rael, not one of them *died. But the heart of Pharaoh was hard, and he did not let the people go.* שְׁמוֹת Exodus 9:6-7

The Plague of Boils

READER 6   *And* ADONAI *said to Moshe... "Take in the fullness of your hands the soot of a furnace," and Moshe sprinkled it towards the heavens before the eyes of Pharaoh. It became small dust over all the land of Egypt, and* both the people and animals of Egypt broke forth with boils and blisters. שְׁמוֹת Exodus 9:8-9

ALL   And it was so—the sixth plague. ADONAI struck Egypt with boils.

READER 6   *But* ADONAI *hardened the heart of Pharaoh, and he [still] would not listen.* Pharaoh still *exalted* himself *against* the *people* of Yis'rael—*so as not to let them go.* שְׁמוֹת Exodus 9:12 & 17

The Plague of Hail

READER 7   ADONAI said to Moshe, "Say to Pharaoh, '*By now I [could] have put forth My hand and slayed you, and you [would have] been wiped from the* face of the *earth! And yet, for this I have caused you to stand: so as to show you My power, and for the sake of declaring My Name in all the earth!'"* שְׁמוֹת Exodus 9:15-16 So ADONAI sent *hail... such as had not been in Egypt, even from the day of its founding.* שְׁמוֹת Exodus 9:18 *And the hail,* mixed with fire, *struck in all the land of Egypt all that was in the field—from man to beast, and every herb... and tree of the field it broke. Only in the land of Goshen, where the sons of Yis'rael lived, was there no hail.* שְׁמוֹת Exodus 9:25-26

ALL   And it was so—the seventh plague. ADONAI struck Egypt with hail.

READER 7   *And Pharaoh sent* for Moshe and said, *"I have sinned this time*—ADONAI *is the Righteous, and I and my people* are *the Wicked. Pray to* ADONAI, *and plead that there be no more thunder of* GOD *and hail, and I [will] let you go..."* So Moshe *went out from Pharaoh... and spread his hands to* ADONAI, *and the thunder and the hail ceased...*

שְׁמוֹת Exodus 9:27-28 & 33

ALL   *[But when] Pharaoh saw that the storms had ceased— the hail and the thunder—he continued to sin, and hardened his heart... and he did not let the sons of Yis'rael go, as* ADONAI *had spoken by the hand of Moshe.*

שְׁמוֹת Exodus 9:34-35

The Plague of Locusts

READER 8   And Moshe went to Pharaoh and said to him, *"This is what* ADONAI, GOD *of the Hebrews, says, 'How long will you refuse to be humbled at My presence? Let My people go, [that] they [may] serve Me. For if you refuse to let My people go, behold, I will bring the locust to your border.... What is left from the hail, they will eat... they will fill your houses, and the houses of all your servants, and the houses of all the Egyptians—it will be unlike any-thing your fathers or your father's fathers have seen...'"*

שְׁמוֹת Exodus 10:3-6

So Pharaoh said to Moshe, *"Go, serve* ADONAI *your* GOD*—[but] who is going with you?"*

Moshe replied, *"[We go] with our young ones, our aged ones, our sons and daughters, our flock and our herd— for we have a feast to* ADONAI.*"*

And Pharaoh answered, *"Only your men may go..."* and Moshe was *cast out from the presence of Pharaoh.*

שְׁמוֹת Exodus 10:8-11

ALL   And it was so—the eighth plague. ADONAI struck Egypt with locusts.

READER 8   The locusts went up against all the land of Egypt... and it covered the eye of all the land, and the land was darkened... and there was not left any green thing in the trees or in the herb of the field, in all the land of Egypt. So Pharaoh called for Moshe and said, "I have sinned against ADONAI your GOD, and against you! And now, bear with my sin, I beg you... and pray to ADONAI your GOD, that He turn aside this death from me." So Moshe prayed to ADONAI, and ADONAI turned a very strong sea wind and it blew all the locusts into the Red Sea. שְׁמוֹת Exodus 10:14-19

ALL   But ADONAI hardened the heart of Pharaoh, and he did not let the sons of Yis'rael go. שְׁמוֹת Exodus 10:20

The Plague of Darkness

READER 9   So ADONAI said to Moshe, "Stretch out your hand towards the heavens, and there will be darkness over the land of Egypt—and the darkness [will be] felt." And there was a thick darkness in all the land of Egypt... they could not see one another, and no one left his place for three days... But to all the sons of Yis'rael, there was light in their dwellings. שְׁמוֹת Exodus 10:21-23

ALL   And it was so—the ninth plague. ADONAI struck Egypt with a thick darkness.

READER 9   And Pharaoh called to Moshe and said, "Go, serve ADONAI, only your flock and your herd must stay." But Moshe replied... "Our cattle must go with us that we may make sacrifices for ADONAI our GOD." But ADONAI hardened the heart of Pharaoh, and he remained unwilling to let them go. Then Pharaoh said to Moshe, "Go from me, and guard yourself—see my face no more—for in the day you see my face again, you die." And Moshe said, "Rightly have you spoken—I will see your face no more." שְׁמוֹת Exodus 10:24-29

Death of the Firstborn

FACILITATOR So Moshe called for all the elders of Yis'rael and said to them, "Draw out and take for yourselves from the flock, for your families... a lamb, a perfect one... from the sheep or the goats... and slaughter the Pesach-sacrifice. Take a bunch of hyssop and dip it in the blood from the sacrifice and strike it on the lintel, and on the two side-posts of your doors, and do not go out from the opening of your houses till morning. When ADONAI passes on to strike the Egyptians, He will see the blood on the lintel... and pass over the opening and not permit the destruction to come into your houses to strike you. שְׁמוֹת Exodus 12:21-23 with 12:5 Nothing will come against all the sons of Yis'rael, so that you will know that ADONAI makes a separation between the Egyptians and Yis'rael." שְׁמוֹת Exodus 11:7

⌒‿⌒‿⌒

CHILDREN'S CRAFT (OPTIONAL—P. 49)

⌒‿⌒‿⌒

And ADONAI said to Moshe, "One more plague will I bring in on Pharaoh, and on Egypt.

ALL Afterwards, he will let you go. שְׁמוֹת Exodus 11:1

FACILITATOR I am going out into the midst of Egypt, שְׁמוֹת Exodus 11:4

ALL and every first-born in the land... will die. שְׁמוֹת Exodus 11:5

FACILITATOR There will be a great cry in all the land of Egypt, such as there has never been before,

ALL and will never be again." שְׁמוֹת Exodus 11:6

FACILITATOR And it came to pass, in the middle [of the night],

ALL that ADONAI struck down every first-born in the land of Egypt.

FACILITATOR *There was a great cry in Egypt, for there was not a house where there was not one dead.* שְׁמוֹת Exodus 12:29-30 So Pharaoh called for Moshe and said,

ALL *"Rise, go out from the midst of my people, both you and the sons of Yis'rael, and go, serve* ADONAI *according to your word.* Take every person and animal that is yours, *as you have spoken, and go, then bless me, too."* שְׁמוֹת Exodus 12:31-32

FACILITATOR *The Egyptians hastened to send Yis'rael out of the land, for they said, "We are all dead."* So the people *took up their dough before it was fermented, and bound up their kneading-troughs in their garments on their shoulders. And* ADONAI *gave the people favor in the eyes of the Egyptians, and they plundered the Egyptians,* asking them for vessels of silver and gold, and garments. The men of Yis'rael alone numbered *six hundred thousand, and a mixed multitude also went up with them.* The *flock and herd,* too, numbered greatly. *And it came to pass... that* after *four hundred and thirty years* to the day, in exactly the way ADONAI told Av'raham it would happen, ADONAI *brought out the sons of Yis'rael from the land of Egypt.* שְׁמוֹת Exodus 12:33-41 & 51

Let us again raise our cup and drink, and rejoice in the salvation of ADONAI!

ALL ברוך אתה יי אלהינו מלך העולם בורא פרי הגפן

Baruch atah ADONAI 'eloheinu melech haolam bo-re p'riy hagafen

Blessed are you, ADONAI our God, King of the Universe, who creates the fruit of the vine.

My strength and song is יָהּ, *Yah, and He has become my* יְשׁוּעָה, *y'shuah (salvation): This is my* GOD, *and I glorify Him;* GOD *of my father—I exalt him!* שְׁמוֹת Exodus 15:2

ALL DRINK JOYFULLY! REFILL CUPS AS NEEDED.

Y'shuat ADONAI
The Salvation of the LORD

FACILITATOR   But that was just the beginning of the salvation of the LORD. ADONAI *went before them by day in a pillar of cloud, to lead them in the way, and by night in a pillar of fire, to give light to them, to go by day and by night. GOD did not lead them the way of the land of the Philistines...* but by the way of the Red Sea.
שְׁמוֹת Exodus 13:21 & 17

READER 1   But *the heart of Pharaoh and of his servants turned against the people* of Yis'rael, *and they said, "What is this we have done? that we have sent Yis'rael away from our service!" And* ADONAI *hardened the heart of Pharaoh king of Egypt, and he pursued the sons of Yis'rael and overtook them, as they encamped by the sea.* שְׁמוֹת Exodus 14:5-9

READER 2   As *Pharaoh drew near, the sons of Yis'rael saw him and feared exceedingly. The sons of Yis'rael cried out to* ADONAI *and said to Moshe, "Because there are no graves in Egypt, you have taken us away to die in a wilderness? What is this you have done to us—to bring us out of Egypt?"* שְׁמוֹת Exodus 14:10-11 *And Moshe said to the people,*

ALL   *"Fear not, still yourselves, and see* יְשׁוּעַת יהוה, *y'shuat* ADONAI*—the salvation of the LORD—which He will do for you today. For as you have seen the Egyptians today, you will never see them again!* ADONAI *will fight for you—you need only to keep silent."* שְׁמוֹת Exodus 14:13-14

READER 3   Then *the Messenger of* GOD, *who went before the camp of Yis'rael, moved and went behind them, and the pillar of the cloud went from their front and stood at their rear, coming in between the camp of the Egyptians and the camp of Yis'rael. And there was cloud and darkness, yet it enlightened the night, and the one did not draw near the other all night long.* שְׁמוֹת Exodus 14:19-20

READER 4   *And Moshe stretched out his hand towards the sea, and ADONAI caused the sea to go on by a strong east wind all the night, and made the sea become dry ground. When the waters had cleaved, the sons of Yis'rael went into the midst of the sea on dry land—the waters were like a wall to them, on their right and on their left.* שְׁמוֹת Exodus 14:21-22

ALL   *With the blast of Your nostrils the waters heaped together. The flowing waters stood as a heap; the depths congealed in the heart of the sea.* שְׁמוֹת Exodus 15:8

READER 5   *The Egyptians pursued them into the midst of the sea, and it came to pass, in the morning watch, that ADONAI looked to the camp of the Egyptians through the pillar of fire and of the cloud, and troubled the camp of the Egyptians. He turned aside the wheels of their chariots and they led them with difficulty. The Egyptians were saying,*

"Let us flee from the face of Yis'rael, for ADONAI *is fighting for them against us!"* שְׁמוֹת Exodus 14:23-25

ALL   *Your right hand,* ADONAI, *has become great in power; Your right hand,* ADONAI, *will crush the enemy.*

שְׁמוֹת Exodus 15:6

READER 6   As ADONAI commanded, Moshe stretched out his hand towards the sea, and the sea turned back, at the turning of the morning, to its normal flow, and the Egyptians fled at its coming. ADONAI shook off the Egyptians in the midst of the sea, and the waters turned back and covered the chariots and the horsemen, even all the force of Pharaoh... not even one of them was left.

שְׁמוֹת Exodus 14:27-28

ALL   *Sing to* ADONAI, *for He has triumphed gloriously! The horse and its rider He has thrown into the sea!*

שְׁמוֹת Exodus 15:21

FACILITATOR   And the sons of Yis'rael went on dry land in the midst of the sea... and ADONAI saved Yis'rael that day out of the hand of the Egyptians. Yis'rael saw the Egyptians dead on the sea-shore, and the great hand with which ADONAI had saved them. שְׁמוֹת Exodus 14:29-31

Let us again lift our cups and rejoice with thanksgiving for what ADONAI has done!

ALL   *For the Egyptians we saw that day, we have never seen them again.* ADONAI *fought for us—we needed only to keep silent."* שְׁמוֹת Exodus 14:13b-14

ברוך אתה יי אלהינו מלך העולם בורא פרי הגפן

Baruch atah ADONAI 'eloheinu melech haolam bo-re p'riy hagafen

Blessed are you, ADONAI our God, King of the Universe, who creates the fruit of the vine.

ALL DRINK JOYFULLY AND EMPTY YOUR CUPS.
(DO NOT REFILL)

Worthy Is the Lamb!

SON   Abba, is that the end of the story?

ABBA   No, my son, it was just the beginning, for the sons of Yis'rael set out that day on a journey that continues even now. Our people have yet to fulfill the covenant ADONAI made with Av'raham to be a blessing to all the nations of the earth.

SON   Abba, how will the covenant be fulfilled?

ABBA   It already began, my son, almost two thousand years ago, when another Pesach was slaughtered, and by *His blood* the sons of Yis'rael—indeed the whole world—were set free!

〜〜〜

FACILITATOR   *And the day... came, on which the Pesach had to be sacrificed. So Yeshua sent* כֵּיפָא, *Keifa and* יוֹחָנָן, *Yochan-an, saying, "Go, prepare the Pesach for us, that we may eat it."* Luke 22:7-8 *When the hour came, Yeshua reclined at the table, and the twelve apostles with Him. And He said to them, "With longing I have desired to eat this Pesach with you before My suffering. For I say to you, that I will eat of it no more until it is fulfilled when the Reign of God comes."* Luke 22:14-16

FACILITATOR LIFTS UP THE MATZOT

And while they were eating, Yeshua took the matzah, blessed ADONAI, broke it, and gave it to the disciples.
מַתִּתְיָהוּ Matthew 26:26

ALL   ברוך אתה יי אלהינו מלך העולם המוציא לחם מן הארץ
Baruch atah ADONAI 'eloheinu melech haolam hamotziy lechem min haaretz

Blessed are you, ADONAI our God, King of the Universe, who brings forth bread from the earth.

FACILITATOR BREAKS THE MATZOT
AND DISTRIBUTES IT TO THE HOUSEHOLD.
(WAIT TO EAT)

FACILITATOR Then Yeshua said,

*"Take, eat, this is My body... that for you is being given.
Do this to remember Me."* מַתִּתְיָהוּ Matthew 26:26, Luke 22:19

ALL EAT MATZAH.

FACILITATOR LIFTS UP THE FRUIT OF THE VINE.

Then Yeshua took the cup, and having given thanks to
ADONAI, *gave some to them.* מַתִּתְיָהוּ Matthew 26:27

ALL ברוך אתה יי אלהינו מלך העולם בורא פרי הגפן
Baruch atah ADONAI 'eloheinu melech haolam bo-re p'riy hagafen

Blessed are you, ADONAI our God, King of the
Universe, who creates the fruit of the vine.

FACILITATOR DISTRIBUTES THE FRUIT OF THE VINE.
(WAIT TO DRINK)

FACILITATOR And Yeshua said,

*"Drink of it—all of you; for this is My blood of
the covenant, that for many is being poured out—
for the release [from the imprisonment] of sins."*
מַתִּתְיָהוּ Matthew 26:27-28

ALL DRINK, REFILL CUPS AS NEEDED.

After singing the הַלֵּל, *Halel, they went forth to*
הַר הַזֵּיתִים, *Har HaZeitiym (the Mount of Olives). "Remain here, and stay awake with Me,"* the Master said
to His disciples. *"Exceedingly sorrowful is My soul—to
death."* מַתִּתְיָהוּ Matthew 26:30 & 38

READER 1 *And having gone a little further, He fell on his face...*
מַתִּתְיָהוּ Matthew 26:39a

READER 2	...*and being in agony, He was praying more earnestly...*
READER 3	...*and His sweat became, as it were, great drops of blood...*
ALL	...*falling upon the ground.* Luke 22:44
FACILITATOR	*Distressed and troubled,* Mark 14:33 Yeshua cried out, saying, *"My Father, if it is possible, let this cup pass from Me...* מַתִּתְיָהוּ Matthew 26:39b
ALL	*"...Yet, not as I will, but as You will."* מַתִּתְיָהוּ Matthew 26:39c
FACILITATOR	*Again, a second time,* and a third, *having gone away, He prayed, saying, "My Father, if this cup cannot pass away from Me unless I drink it...*
ALL	*"...Your will be done."* מַתִּתְיָהוּ Matthew 26:42
READER 4	Then, *the Son of Man...*
READER 5	betrayed *with a kiss...* Luke 22:48
READER 6	was seized and deserted...
ALL	...in the *hour and the power of the darkness...* Luke 22:53
FACILITATOR	*He was despised, and rejected of men— a man of pains, and acquainted with sickness.* יְשַׁעְיָהוּ Isaiah 53:3a
ALL	*As one hiding his face from us, he was despised, and we esteemed him not.* יְשַׁעְיָהוּ Isaiah 53:3b
FACILITATOR	*Surely our sicknesses he bore, and our pains— he carried them.* יְשַׁעְיָהוּ Isaiah 53:4a
ALL	*And we—we have esteemed him stricken, smitten of GOD, and afflicted.* יְשַׁעְיָהוּ Isaiah 53:4b

FACILITATOR	*And he was pierced for our transgressions,* *bruised for our iniquities.* יְשַׁעְיָהוּ Isaiah 53:5a
ALL	*The chastisement of our peace is on him,* *and by his bruise there is healing to us.* יְשַׁעְיָהוּ Isaiah 53:5b
FACILITATOR	*All of us like sheep have wandered,* *each to his own way we have turned.* יְשַׁעְיָהוּ Isaiah 53:6a
ALL	*And* ADONAI *has laid on him* *the punishment of us all.* יְשַׁעְיָהוּ Isaiah 53:6b
FACILITATOR	*He was oppressed, and he was humbled, and he* *opened not his mouth. As a lamb to the slaughter he* *was brought.* יְשַׁעְיָהוּ Isaiah 53:7a
ALL	*And as a sheep before its shearers is silenced,* *he opened not his mouth.* יְשַׁעְיָהוּ Isaiah 53:7b
READER 1	They stripped Him naked...
READER 2	...and put on Him a scarlet robe.
READER 3	They put on His head a crown made of thorns,
READER 4	...and kneeled before Him, mocking Him.
READER 5	They spat on Him,
READER 6	...and struck Him repeatedly on His head,
READER 7	...then led Him away to crucify Him. מַתִּתְיָהוּ Matthew 27:28-31
FACILITATOR	*And darkness came over all the land, and the sun was* *darkened, and the curtain of the Temple was torn in* *two.* Luke 23:45 *And having cried out with a loud voice,* *Yeshua said at last,*
ALL	*"Father, into Your hands I commit My spirit!"* Luke 23:46

FACILITATOR Then the Messiah Yeshua *breathed His last* Luke 23:46 and *died for our sins, according to the Scriptures.* 1Corinthians 15:3

ALL But that was just the beginning of the salvation of the LORD!

FACILITATOR *He was buried and rose on the third day....* 1Corinthians 15:4 *...so we also might walk in newness of life.* Romans 6:4 It was He *Himself who bore our sins in His body upon the tree, so that we having died to our sins, may live to righteousness; for by His bruises we were healed.* כֵּיפָא א 1Peter 2:24

ALL *With Messiah I have been crucified, and no more do I live, but Messiah lives in me! And that which I now live in the flesh, I live in the faith of the Son of God, who loved me and gave Himself for me!* Galatians 2:20

FACILITATOR We have been *redeemed... with the precious blood, as of a lamb unblemished and unspotted—Messiah's...* כֵּיפָא א 1Peter 1:18-19 *Therefore, let us clean out the old leaven, that we may be a new batch, just as we are* already, *in reality, unleavened. For also our Pesach was sacrificed for us—Messiah! so that we may keep the feast, not with old leaven, nor with the leaven of evil and wickedness, but with the matzah of sincerity and truth.* 1Corinthians 5:7-8

ALL STAND, HOLDING CUPS.

His Loving-kindness
Endures Forever!

תְּהִלִּים Psalm 136 (without verses 17-20)

FACILITATOR	Give thanks to ADONAI, for He is good!
ALL	כִּי לְעוֹלָם חַסְדּוֹ, *kiy l'olam chas'do!*
	(His loving-kindness endures forever.)

FACILITATOR	Give thanks to the GOD of gods!
ALL	כִּי לְעוֹלָם חַסְדּוֹ, *kiy l'olam chas'do!*

FACILITATOR	Give thanks to the Lord of lords!
ALL	כִּי לְעוֹלָם חַסְדּוֹ, *kiy l'olam chas'do!*

FACILITATOR	To Him who *does great wonders by Himself alone,*
ALL	כִּי לְעוֹלָם חַסְדּוֹ, *kiy l'olam chas'do!*

FACILITATOR	To Him who *made the heavens with understanding,*
ALL	כִּי לְעוֹלָם חַסְדּוֹ, *kiy l'olam chas'do!*

FACILITATOR	To Him who *spreads the earth over the waters,*
ALL	כִּי לְעוֹלָם חַסְדּוֹ, *kiy l'olam chas'do!*

FACILITATOR	To Him who *made the great lights,*
ALL	כִּי לְעוֹלָם חַסְדּוֹ, *kiy l'olam chas'do!*

FACILITATOR	The sun *to rule by day,*
ALL	כִּי לְעוֹלָם חַסְדּוֹ, *kiy l'olam chas'do!*

FACILITATOR	The moon and stars *to rule by night,*
ALL	כִּי לְעוֹלָם חַסְדּוֹ, *kiy l'olam chas'do!*

FACILITATOR	To Him who *struck Egypt in their first-born,*
ALL	כִּי לְעוֹלָם חַסְדּוֹ, *kiy l'olam chas'do!*

FACILITATOR	And brought forth *Yis'rael from their midst,*
ALL	כִּי לְעוֹלָם חַסְדּוֹ, *kiy l'olam chas'do!*

FACILITATOR	By a strong hand, *and an out-stretched arm,*
ALL	כִּי לְעוֹלָם חַסְדּוֹ, *kiy l'olam chas'do!*

FACILITATOR	To Him who *cut the sea of Suf into parts,*
ALL	כִּי לְעוֹלָם חַסְדּוֹ, *kiy l'olam chas'do!*

FACILITATOR	*And caused Yis'rael to pass through its midst,*
ALL	כִּי לְעוֹלָם חַסְדּוֹ, *kiy l'olam chas'do!*

FACILITATOR	*And shook out Pharaoh and his force in the sea of Suf,*
ALL	כִּי לְעוֹלָם חַסְדּוֹ, *kiy l'olam chas'do!*

FACILITATOR	*To Him who led His people in the wilderness,*
ALL	כִּי לְעוֹלָם חַסְדּוֹ, *kiy l'olam chas'do!*

FACILITATOR	*And gave His people their land as an inheritance,*
ALL	כִּי לְעוֹלָם חַסְדּוֹ, *kiy l'olam chas'do!*

FACILITATOR	*An inheritance to Yis'rael His servant.*
ALL	כִּי לְעוֹלָם חַסְדּוֹ, *kiy l'olam chas'do!*

FACILITATOR	*Who in our lowliness has remembered us*
ALL	כִּי לְעוֹלָם חַסְדּוֹ, *kiy l'olam chas'do!*

FACILITATOR	*And He delivered us from our enemies.*
ALL	כִּי לְעוֹלָם חַסְדּוֹ, *kiy l'olam chas'do!*

FACILITATOR	*Giving food to all flesh,*
ALL	כִּי לְעוֹלָם חַסְדּוֹ, *kiy l'olam chas'do!*

FACILITATOR	*Give thanks to the GOD of the heavens!*
ALL	כִּי לְעוֹלָם חַסְדּוֹ, *kiy l'olam chas'do!*

ALL DRINK JOYFULLY, AND EMPTY YOUR CUPS!

FACILITATOR	Let us now "keep the feast" with joy and celebration, remembering how the *Pesach* was sacrificed on our behalf. Let us recall our salvation that came by the shedding of innocent blood, and how, with a mighty hand and an outstretched arm, we have been redeemed from bondage forever!

ALL	*Worthy is the Lamb that was slain to receive power, and riches, and wisdom, and strength, and honor, and glory, and blessing!* Revelation 5:12 *Behold, the Lamb of God, who is taking away the sin of the world!* יוֹחָנָן John 1:29

אָמֵן, AMEN!

Changing the Way We "Do" Passover

This supplement to *Behold the Lamb* has been provided to help you better understand some of the background of the traditional Passover seder, as well as offer suggestions for a meaningful, Scripture-based, celebration of this special moment on Israel's annual calendar. The following pages contain information on several different topics, illuminating some of the finer points of Passover—points which are usually missed in both conventional and Messianic observance.

For additional suggestions, or if you plan to facilitate this *'avodah*, please read the *Behold the Lamb Preparation Guide*, which is available separately.

With Respect to Tradition

Reinventing the Passover Haggadah[1] is a long-lived, time-honored, Jewish tradition. Yet with each new Haggadah—including those of the Messianic persuasion—the essence of the Talmudic Passover seder[2] has gone unchanged... until now. *Behold the Lamb* may be just another Messianic Haggadah, but it is distinguished in part by its atypical approach to Jewish tradition. Indeed, as described in the preface, this *'avodah* is not offered as a *revision* of the *seder*, but as an *alternative* memorial of the Passover sacrifice. As such, *Behold the Lamb* draws not upon centuries of acknowledged *tradition*, but from the eternal source of all perfect truth—the Word of ADONAI, *the Scriptures*.

Why make such a dramatic departure from the accepted norm? Is this a display of arrogance toward—or worse, ignorance of—Jewish culture and tradition? On the contrary,

> The traditions and cultures of the Judaisms have developed over the course of many centuries, becoming inseparable from Jewish holiday observances. And yet—despite their beauty, apparent wisdom, and sometimes near-universal acceptance—we as disciples of Messiah have an obligation to at least *reconsider* these traditions in light of Scripture.
>
> With the utmost respect for our Jewish people and regard for our rich cultural heritage, we have nevertheless chosen a "Scripture-first" approach to understanding and keeping the

Mo'adiym. In so doing, our goal is not to *denigrate* or *exclude* tradition—rather to *elevate Scripture* and allow the *power of the Word* to exercise its authority in our lives.[3]

Nowhere is this value more highly upheld than in *Behold the Lamb*—a telling of the Passover story that consists almost entirely of quotations from Scripture. Only in pursuit of the simple and clear Word of God did tradition fail to find a substantial voice in our *'avodah.*[4]

Lest we lament the absence of such traditions, let us consider, for example, the content of the traditional seder's centerpiece: the *seder plate.* The concept of the plate itself is ascriptural... and unfortunately, so are all *but one* of its elements. The bitter herbs alone[5] pass Scriptural muster, while the remaining ingredients find their origins in a mixture of innovation, substitution, and—sadly—paganism.[6] Yet despite this reality, the character of the seder has gone largely unquestioned. Is this the kind of tradition—cherished though it may be—upon which our remembrance of the Passover should be established?

The traditional seder surely holds an esteemed place in the annals of Judaism; yet reimagining it in each generation is not only within our purview, it is apparently expected. As disciples of Messiah and the righteous remnant of Israel, however, our goal cannot be the absent-minded perpetuation of dubious ceremonies and rites—no matter how *Jewish* they may be, or how *Messianic* we make them. Instead, our goal must be a return to the simple, unrefined Word of God—pure and unchanged by the hands of time... magnified and immutable in the minds of men.

The seder plate—counter-clockwise, beginning with the roasted egg (*zeroa*), *karpas* (usually parsley), *charoset* (sweet apple and nut mixture), *chazeret* (bitter herb #1), *maror* (usually horseradish, bitter herb #2), and shankbone. Other traditional elements of the seder table include salt water (sometimes placed in the center of the seder plate, sometimes in place of the *chazeret*), the four cups (fruit of the vine), and the *afikomen* (a portion of matzah).

Unraveling the Mystery of Matzah

Bread is not only the staff of life, it is a staple for Passover; and in this case, it is *unleavened* bread—or *matzah*—that concerns us. Indeed, the prospect of being *oppressed* for an entire week by the flavorless "bread of affliction"[7] is what often *concerns* adherents the most. So why do we torment ourselves with a substance as banal as kosher-for-passover matzah? Because it is forbidden by Rabbinic halachah to make tasty passover matzah. In fact, there are stringent rules concerning both its ingredients *and* production. One Rabbi encapsulates it this way:

> Matzah is no more than flour and cold water—no more. If the mixture of flour and water is allowed to stand for more than a minimum time of 18 minutes, it is in that time acted upon by an external process which begins to intercede. Yeast bacteria which are found in the air, multiply causing fermentation. The yeast microorganisms are an uninvited invading army intruding on the flour and water mixture helping themselves to a delicious meal of sugar molecules. As the yeast microorganisms multiply by the billions they release carbon dioxide gas that sours the dough.[8]

Does Scripture agree? Let's start with the make-up of matzah. Exodus 29:2 says,

> ...and unleavened bread, and cakes unleavened **mingled with oil**, and wafers unleavened **spread with oil**; of fine wheaten flour shalt thou make them. JPS *(author's emphasis)*

So, according to Torah, *matzah* is in *no way* "no more than flour and cold water." On the contrary, there are three types of matzah listed in this verse[9]—

- "unleavened bread"—לֶחֶם מַצּוֹת, *lechem matzot* (matzah-bread)

- "cakes unleavened"—חַלֹּת מַצֹּת, *chalot matzot* (matzah-challah)

- "wafers unleavened"—רְקִיקֵי מַצּוֹת, *r'qiyqei matzot* (matzah-crackers)

—and *two* of them include *oil*,[10] either *mixed in* with the flour, or *spread* (literally, "anointed") on the surface.

Now let's unravel the rest of this matzah mystery: Does matzah need to be made within eighteen minutes of making the dough—the "mixture of flour and water"? You be the judge.

According to Exodus 12:33-39,

> ...the Egyptians were urgent upon the people, to send them out of the land in haste... And the people took their **dough before it was leavened**,[11] their kneading-troughs being bound up in their clothes upon their shoulders... And the children of Israel journeyed from Rameses to Succoth, about six hundred thousand men on foot, beside children... And **they baked unleavened cakes of the dough which they brought forth out of Egypt, for it was not leavened**; because they were thrust out of Egypt, and could not tarry, neither had they prepared for themselves any victual. JPS *(author's emphasis)*

It is difficult to imagine Moses halting the exodus seventeen minutes into the journey, in order to stop, drop, and bake rabbinically-kosher matzah! Of course, human ingenuity can tell us precisely when airborne yeast microorganisms are able to activate our unleavened dough. Nevertheless, it should be obvious that the sons of Israel were not expected to remove the שְׂאֹר, *s'or*[12] from the *air* as well as their homes.

See **Esther's Matzah Recipes** on page 45 for delicious, homemade matzah!

The eating of matzah is meant to *remind* us of how we were afflicted in Egypt—not to become the *source* of our affliction! Store-bought Passover Matzah is prepared on matzah-making machines[13] under strict rabbinical supervision; anyone concerned with submitting to that authority should look no further than their local supermarket shelves. But if you desire to be liberated from the bonds of bland unleavened bread, here is the permission you need... a feast-worthy alternative awaits your kitchen's creation![14]

Keeping Vigil—A Lost Command

When comparing the myriad of Passover traditions with the instructions of Scripture, one of the most meaningful paradigm shifts we encounter is that there is no *day* of Passover. A Feast? For sure.[15] An appointed time? Absolutely.[16] But a *day?* Scripture clearly teaches to the contrary.

Indeed, the appointed time begins with the sacrifice of the Passover on the fourteenth of the first month **at sundown**.[17] After cooking the sacrifice, it must then be consumed—eaten, or burned up— by dawn.[18] With the break of day comes the Feast of Matzah—a closely related, yet distinct set of appointed times—which commemorates the day Israel set out from Egypt: "on the *fifteenth* day of the first month, on the *day after*[19] the Passover" (Numbers 33:3, *author's emphasis*). In short, the Passover is the sacrifice itself, it's slaughter is at *sundown,* and it must be cooked and consumed before morning. Passover is not a *day* at all[20]—if anything, it lasts only for a *nighttime!*

Such an understanding of Passover's character immediately illuminates several previously obscured passages of Scripture, beginning with Exodus 12:42. Referring to the night of the first Passover, it says,

> [Because] it *was* for ADONAI a night of keeping vigil (to bring them out from the land of Egypt), it *is* this night for all the sons of ישְׂרָאֵל, *Yis'rael* [a night] of keeping vigil (to [honor] ADONAI)— to their generations.

All night long during that first Passover, ADONAI guarded Israel with vigilance. He "passed over" the houses of the sons of Israel, while—outside their protected doors—death secured their salvation. In remembrance of this event and of ADONAI's mighty hand of deliverance, the night of Passover is to also be "for all the sons of Yis'rael [a night] of keeping vigil... to their generations"—a time to remember the first Passover by *remaining awake* and *keeping watch* in honor of ADONAI our God.

Though Scripture does not explicitly expound on how such a "Passover Vigil"[21] might look, consider Matthew 26:38-46 (cf.

Mark 14:32-42; Luke 22:39-46), when the Master Yeshua Himself entered Gethsemane on the night of *His* last Passover:

> Then [Yeshua] said to them, "Exceedingly sorrowful is my soul—to death. Remain here and [stay] **awake**[22] **with Me.**" And having gone forward a little, He fell on His face, praying, and saying, "My Father! If it is possible, let this cup pass from me! Nevertheless, not as I will, but as You [will]." And He came to the disciples, and **found them sleeping,** and He said to כֵּיפָא, Keifa, **"So! You were not able to [stay] awake with me [for] one hour! [Stay] awake, and pray,** that you may not enter into temptation: the spirit, indeed, is willing, but the flesh [is] weak." Again, a second time, having gone away, He prayed, saying, "My Father, if this cup cannot pass away from me unless I drink it, Your will be done!" And having come [back], **He found them sleeping again, for their eyes were heavy.** And having left them, having gone away again, He prayed a third time, saying the same word, then He came [back] to His disciples and said to them, "Sleep from now on, and rest! Look! the hour has come near, and the Son of Man is handed over to the hands of sinners. Rise, let us go! Look! he who is handing Me over [in betrayal] has come near." *(author's emphasis)*

Surely, the Master was in distress; and we might reasonably expect Him to desire His disciples' company in such an hour of need. But what if that is not the only subtext underscoring this passage? Is it possible that the Master—in profound recognition of His role as the *ultimate* Passover sacrifice—was also soberly recalling the *first* Passover sacrifice in keeping with Exodus 12:42? From His own mouth, we hear the Master commanding His disciples, "[stay] awake with Me;" and later, upon finding them asleep, saying, "[Stay] awake, and pray." Could this be the account of Yeshua's own "Passover Vigil?" Did the Master want His disciples to stay awake not simply to attend to Him, or be on the watch for evildoers, but so that they could see and remember how the Passover sacrifice would once again save all Israel?

With the above Scriptures in mind, the backdrop for an unforgettable, all-night Passover experience—the "Passover Vigil"—is set. At sundown, we commence with the *Pesach 'Avodah*, remembering how ADONAI set us free from slavery in Egypt, and how the blood of the Messiah Yeshua—our Passover Lamb—set us free from bondage to sin and death. At the conclusion of the 'Avodah, in joyful, resounding praise, we enter fully into the Feast—with matzah, maror, and all manner of delicacy—thankful for the abundant and ever-present provision of our Master and Savior. As the meal unceremoniously dissipates and we settle in for the night ahead, we eagerly await the rising of the sun, and the coming of the commemorative day of our deliverance. Throughout the night: we eat matzah (and more!), recalling the reality of our unleavenedness in Messiah; we pray, as the Master exhorted His disciples, so that we will not soon fall again into temptation; and we keep vigil, remaining physically and spiritually awake, in honor of the vigil that our Father once kept for us. As we celebrate and feast in the company of our loved ones, joy and laughter urge us on toward wakefulness. With light hearts and heavy eyes, we inevitably drift off to sleep, waking now and then to the happy sights and sounds of family and close friends keeping vigil on behalf of all.

Removing the Leaven

The sons of Israel are not only commanded to eat matzah during Passover and the Feast of Matzah,[23] but to fast from leaven—indeed, "leaven is not [even to be] found in your houses."[24] According to Jewish tradition, the practice of removing the leaven from the home commences no later than the day before the Passover, culminating in the final search for leaven (bedikat chametz). This practice is designed to ensure that no leaven is found in the home during the Passover and the ensuing seven-day feast. Indeed, especially in our modern world of spacious living, refrigeration, and climate-controlled storage, there is often a great deal of leaven to remove—and many hidden places in which to find it.[25] In agreement with the tradition, it is therefore highly advisable to make a grand sweep of one's home before the Passover with the intent to remove all our leaven.

Unfortunately, the Torah throws a tiny wrench in this otherwise innovative plan to remove all the leaven before Passover, stating plainly in Exodus 12:15,

[For] seven days, eat matzah. **On the very first day** [*after* the Passover], **cause** [**the**] **leaven to be removed** out of your houses...
(*author's emphasis*)

Scripture makes it absolutely clear that no leaven may be *eaten*, beginning the evening *before* the first day of Matzah, corresponding with the onset of Passover (Ex. 12:18). Yet the *removal* of leaven, according to Torah, is to occur *on the next day*. What makes this chronology even more difficult to reconcile is the equally clear command of Exodus 12:19,

[For] **seven days**, leaven (שְׂאֹר, *s'or*) is not [to be] found in your houses...[26] (*author's emphasis*)

Thus, the conundrum: leaven is to be removed from our homes *on the first day*—the day *after* the Passover—yet we are not to have any leaven in our possession *for seven days* (presumably, beginning the morning of the first day of Matzah)! It is certainly something of a temporal puzzle, and not one for which Jewish tradition has a ready answer. Fortunately, since the Hebrew reckoning of time allows for a *portion* of a day to be counted as "a day,"[27] there may be a viable solution. Here is one set of practical suggestions for how we might reconcile these apparently conflicting commands:

1. Sometime before the Passover (allowing yourself ample time for a thorough house-cleaning), remove *most* of the leaven from your home.[28]

2. At the same time, set aside a manageable portion of leaven or leavened things to *keep* until the first day of the Feast, *after* the Passover. A loaf of bread, for instance, would be appropriate.

3. From the time Passover begins at sunset on the fourteenth of the first month, eat only matzah, according to the Scriptures.[29]

4. At dawn the next morning—upon the conclusion of your "Passover Vigil" (see page 37)—ceremoniously remove the remaining, symbolic portion of leaven from your home.

With this practice, no leaven is found in the home for the vast majority of the first day of Matzah, *and* its final removal has been accomplished *on the first day*. From a memorial standpoint, the next-day-removal of leaven also aids in the remembrance: Israel remained in Egypt for one, final night, and then the following morning, took their first steps out of Egypt toward a new, unleavened freedom!

The ceremonial removal of leaven may consist of an outdoor gathering of the whole household,[30] in which everyone is given a portion of the remaining leaven. Upon lighting a fire[31] and reading aloud from the *Messianic Mo'adiym Devotional*, each person can then cast his portion of leaven into the fire, symbolically beginning his seven-day walk of deliberately practicing sinlessness—the spiritual theme of the week of Matzah.[32]

Since the day after Passover is a no-work day (except for the preparation of food), as well as a holy convocation,[33] you might choose to continue feasting with a refreshing breakfast before moving on with your day—be it in additional celebration, or simply returning home.[34] Indeed, after such an eventful night to remember, it may be a nice, long *nap* that is in order....

Notes

1   "haggadah" means "telling"

2   "seder" means "service"

3   Kevin Geoffrey, *Messianic Mo'adiym Devotional* (Phoenix, AZ: Perfect Word Publishing, 2007), 144.

4   Indeed, only the traditional blessings over the bread and fruit of the vine found their way into the service.

5   The bitter herbs—Scripture literally speaks of מְרֹרִים, m'roriym, plural for מָרֹר, maror—effectively enjoys *two representations* on the plate in the form of maror and a second kind of "bitter herb," the chazeret.

6   For example, the shankbone is a *substitution* for the Passover sacrifice itself, and the charoset is primarily an edible teaching device intended to aid in the telling. It is also difficult to escape the dubious origins of the egg, which, in pagan cultures, "is a symbol of fertility and renewal." George Robinson, *Essential Judaism* (New York: Pocket Books, 2000), 122.

7   Deuteronomy 16:3

8 Rabbi Pinchas Stolper, "The Inner Meaning of Matzah," The Orthodox Union, http://www.ou.org/chagim/pesach/inner.htm (accessed January 8, 2010).

9 cf. Leviticus 2:4-6, 7:12; Numbers 6:15; 1Chronicles 23:29

10 presumably, olive oil

11 "their dough before it was leavened," that is, חָמֵץ, chametz—what dough becomes when it has been leavened.

12 שְׂאֹר, s'or—leavening agent, i.e. yeast. The fact of the matter is that it takes days, not minutes to capture enough airborne yeast to create a "starter" capable of being used to leaven bread. How much more difficult would be the spontaneous leavening of a completed batch of dough made from just flour and water alone (for an example of sourdough starter, see http://www. frugalvillage.com/sourdough.shtml).

13 "Why are most matzot square? Originally, all matzot were shaped round [Exodus 12:39 explicitly references עֻגֹת מַצּוֹת, ugot matzot—"discs of matzah"]. In 1875, a matza-baking machine that made square matzot was invented in England. The machine was subsequently introduced into the United States." Alfred J. Kolatch, The Jewish Book of Why (New York: Jonathan David Publishers, Inc., 1995), 192. Why are the matzot "striped"? It is a result of the machine's manufacturing process.

14 Pastas and rice—anything that "puffs up"—is also rabbinically forbidden on Passover, while kosher-for-passover baking mixes that contain chemical leavening agents (such as baking powder or baking soda) are permitted. What's wrong with this picture? Our advice? Have your lasagna or macaroni & cheese, but not your kosher-for-passover cake, too! (See note 28 for more on chemical leavening agents.)

15 Exodus 34:25

16 Numbers 9:2

17 Exodus 12:6; Leviticus 23:5; Numbers 9:5, 28:16; Deuteronomy 16:6

18 Exodus 12:10, 34:25

19 The traditional Jewish understanding of a "day" is that it is a 24-hour period, running from evening to evening. Since space does not permit an exhaustive treatment of this topic, I will simply state that I do not believe Scripture agrees with the traditional reckoning of a "day." Indeed, in my assessment of Scripture, יוֹם, yom is typically not a 24-hour period beginning at evening or any other time, but rather, "daytime"—the hours between dawn and dusk.

As a brief test case, consider the chronology of Passover/Matzah. According to the traditional reckoning (this gets confusing, so hold on!), "the fifteenth day of the first month" (the first day of Matzah) begins almost simultaneously with the fourteenth of the first month at sundown (when the Passover is sacrificed). But how, I ask, could the sons of Israel have set out from Egypt "on the day after the Passover" if Passover and "the fifteenth day of the first month" commenced at virtually the same moment?

To put it more clearly, how can Passover and the first day of Matzah occupy the same span of time, when Scripture clearly states that one happens *after* the other? On the contrary, Israel left Egypt on the fifteenth day*time* of the first month, the day*time after* the Passover, which had ended by dawn.

[20] Why does Judaism teach that the first day of the Feast of Matzah *is* the "day" of Passover (or that the seven-day Feast of Matzah may also be called the Feast of Passover)? There is no doubt that the Feast of Passover and the Feast of Matzah are closely linked in the Scriptures, and not just because of their chronological proximity to one another. Their complementary commands concerning abstention from leaven and the eating of matzah also blurs the lines of distinction, in one sense. There are also several passages of Scripture which, at first glance, contribute to muddying the waters of understanding—though thoughtful analysis can reconcile them with the plain instructions of Torah (for a discussion of these passages, please visit http://passover.perfect-word.org).

In the end, the most likely explanation for how Passover came to be known in Judaism as a "day" is *convenience*—shorthand. With the two feasts being so closely related—chronologically as well as thematically—human reasoning finds it convenient to assign them a single label. Once our minds turn the week of Matzah into "the week of Passover," it naturally follows that the first day of the feast mistakenly becomes "the *day* of Passover."

[21] It is interesting to note that while a "Passover Vigil" appears to be absent from Judaism's collective consciousness, the general concept of an all-night vigil is not at all foreign to Judaism. Though prescribed nowhere in Scripture, "Tikkun Layl Shavuot" is the traditional, night-long Torah/Talmud study on the night of Shavuot, the Feast of Weeks.

[22] Most translations say "keep watch" or similar, but the greek (γρηγορέω, *gregoreo*) may also be translated "stay awake" or similar, as in 1Th.5:10.

[23] Exodus 12:18; Leviticus 23:6

[24] Exodus 12:19-20

[25] Common places where leaven may be found around the home: under the refrigerator/stove; toaster; microwave; crumbs in the refrigerator/freezer; spills/crumbs in cabinets/drawers; garbage cans; under couches and cushions; in your car; or anywhere food may have been eaten or taken.

[26] cf. Exodus 13:7, "Matzah is to be eaten [for] the seven days, but **no leavened thing is [to be] seen with you**; yes, leaven is not [to be] seen with you **in all your territory**." *(author's emphasis)*

[27] cf. Genesis 42:17-20 and 1Kings 20:29.

[28] What is leaven (חָמֵץ, *chametz*)? Anything made with שְׂאֹר, *s'or* (yeast) has been leavened—this would include all regular bread and bread products. But what about items containing *chemical* leavening agents, such as baking soda (sodium bicarbonate) and baking powder? While not *technically* שְׂאֹר, *s'or*, their real-world function is, nevertheless, *leavening*. When you add a chemical leavening agent to flour and water, it does virtually the same thing that yeast does—it will cause the dough to *rise*.

"Kosher-for-passover" baking mixes, which contain chemical leavening agents, exist for the express intent of making foods that you would normally create with flour, water, and yeast—i.e. something *leavened*. Since, rabbinically speaking, it is forbidden to use flour during the Feast, the way "kosher-for-passover" baking mixes "solve" this dilemma is by substituting regular flour for finely-ground matzah meal (because, since matzah meal has already been baked, it cannot *spontaneously* leaven like flour *allegedly* can—see note 12) and causing it to rise with the addition of chemical leaveners. So, even though these mixes result in an *artificially* leavened product, to some, the use of chemical leavening agents does not *technically* violate the command to avoid leaven. Does this sound "kosher" to you?

If not, then in addition to removing baking soda, baking powder, *and* yeast from your home, you will also want to carefully check the ingredient lists of products that may contain chemical leaveners, such as: "kosher-for-passover" mixes (for cakes, muffins, etc.); seasoning mixes; pre-packaged foods (including vegetarian meat substitutes); alcoholic beverages (unless they say "Kosher for Passover"); pet foods (and some cat litters); some toothpastes and other bath products; deodorizers (for shoes, carpets, feminine products, etc.); some laundry and dishwasher detergents; and anything made by "Arm & Hammer." (What about autolyzed yeast extract or deactivated yeast [brewer's yeast, nutritional yeast, etc.]? It's fermentation power has been rendered inert, so is it still שְׂאֹר, *s'or*? You decide.)

Practically speaking, you can make the removal of leaven a source of stress, a point of legalism, or an exercise in sanctification and self-discipline—it's up to you. Of course, I recommend the latter, and I can tell you from experience that if you do it with the right heart, it becomes more meaningful every year.

29 There is no prohibition about having leaven in one's possession during the night of Passover—the commands of Exodus 12:19-20 and 13:7 go into effect the following morning. As such, there is no conflict of commands, as long as there is no *eating* of leaven, once the sun goes down.

30 An outdoor gathering would be quite appropriate, considering the Passover command to remain indoors until morning (Ex. 12:22).

31 ...or meeting around one that had been burning through the night—as would be the case in order to ensure the consumption of the Passover before dawn (Exodus 12:10, 34:25). For the sake of discussion, the prohibition against lighting a fire on the seventh-day Shabbat does not apply here, since the first day of Matzah is not a Shabbat according to Scripture (though it is a "no-work" day). That said, if Passover should fall on an Erev Shabbat, the same fire used throughout the night to cook and consume the Passover could simply be left to smolder upon daybreak and then used for the destruction of any remaining leaven, thus avoiding a Shabbat violation.

32 For a more complete explanation of the spiritual themes for all the annual appointed times, see the appendix to the *Messianic Mo'adiym Devotional*.

33 Exodus 12:16

34 Deuteronomy 16:7

Matzah Recipes

*Set yourself free from the bonds of bland un-
leavened bread, and enjoy Esther's take on various ways to make matzah. See page 35 for more
about Unraveling the Mystery of Matzah.*

Esther's Delicious Matzah-Crackers

A great tasting substitute for the crunchy, cracker-like, store-bought Matzah

    2 cups flour   ¼ cup vegetable shortening
    1 tsp salt   ¾ cup milk

1. Preheat oven to 425 degrees. A pizza stone preheated in the oven yields best results.

2. Combine flour and salt; and then cut in the shortening (using a hand-held pastry blender or two knives).

3. Pour in milk, stir, and then mix with hands until completely combined.

4. Place dough on a smooth surface (counter top, large wooden cutting board, silicone pastry mat, etc.) very lightly dusted with flour. Knead until smooth.

5. Divide dough into eight equal pieces.

6. Roll each piece into an extremely thin 10 inch circle (keep the rest covered with a moist towel or paper towel until needed).

7. Prick entire surface with a fork.

8. Lift dough very carefully and place in oven on pizza stone or pan.

9. Bake for two minutes (dough will form small bubbles), and then flip. Bake two more minutes until lightly browned.

10. Serve immediately, or cool on a rack and store in a zip-top bag.

 For more Passover and Matzah recipes (plus Gluten-Free substitutes) go to **http://passover.perfect-word.org**

Esther's Flat Bread Matzah-Challah

This fantastic matzah is not crunchy like Esther's Delicious, but is soft like many kinds of flat breads. We usually season this one like Italian flat bread, complete with a seasoned olive oil mixture for dipping.

- 2½ cups flour
- 1 tsp salt
- ¼ tsp garlic powder*
- 2 tsp Italian seasoning*
- ⅓ cup olive oil
- ⅔ cup warm water

1. Preheat oven to 425 degrees. A pizza stone preheated in the oven yields best results.

2. Combine flour, salt, garlic powder and seasoning.

3. Mix in oil with fingers until dough looks like coarse crumbs.

4. Pour in warm water, stir, and then mix with hands until combined.

5. Place dough on a smooth surface (counter top, large wooden cutting board, silicone pastry mat, etc.) very lightly dusted with flour. Knead until smooth.

6. Divide dough into eight equal pieces. Roll each piece into a thin 8 inch circle (keep the rest covered with a moist towel or paper towel until needed).

7. Prick entire surface with fork.

8. Lift dough very carefully and place in oven on pizza stone or pan.

9. Bake for two minutes (dough will form small bubbles), and then flip. Bake two more minutes until very lightly browned.

10. Place on plate and cover with damp cloth, or place directly into a zip-top bag. Serve warm.

Our family enjoys eating this matzah with seasoned olive oil. Just add crushed garlic, black pepper, oregano, or any other combination of spices you like to some extra virgin olive oil, and pour onto a small plate for dipping.

*optional

Esther's Incredible Matzah Toffee

Wow! Nobody doesn't like Esther's Incredible Matzah Toffee...
and soooo easy to make (even Kevin can do it)!

- 1 cup (2 sticks) butter (not margarine)
- 1 cup sugar
- store-bought matzah *(or GF Boxed-Matzah Substitute, see website)*
- 1 bag (2 cups) semi-sweet chocolate chips

1. Preheat oven to 350 degrees.

2. Cover 10 x 15 jelly roll pan with a complete layer of broken matzah pieces.

3. Put butter and sugar in a small pot over medium heat (do not melt butter first), and bring to a boil, stirring frequently.

4. Boil for three minutes, stirring constantly.

5. Evenly pour butter and sugar mixture over matzah pieces.

6. Bake for 12-15 minutes until golden brown and bubbly. (If you remove the pan from the oven before you see a rich golden color, the toffee will have a grainy texture.)

7. Remove pan from oven and immediately sprinkle chocolate chips over the entire surface.

8. Wait one to two minutes, and then evenly spread the melted chocolate with a spatula or knife.

9. Put pan in freezer for 20 minutes. After removing from the freezer, you should be able to lift the toffee from the pan in one entire sheet. If necessary, use a butter knife under the edges to remove toffee from pan.

10. Break toffee into pieces, and enjoy!

11. Store in a zip-top bag in freezer or refrigerator.

Children's
Craft

[YOU WERE] REDEEMED... WITH PRECIOUS BLOOD, AS OF
A LAMB UNBLEMISHED AND UNSPOTTED—MESSIAH'S...

כֵּיפָא א 1Peter 1:18-19

Meet "HaSeh," the Passover Lamb!

"HaSeh" is a small, cotton-ball lamb replica containing a pouch of homemade corn-syrup "blood." During the 'avodah, HaSeh is used as a teaching picture of a sacrifice—his "blood" being applied to the doorposts of each child's "house" (below).

The "house" is a coloring/drawing page with craft stick door-posts. Before the 'avodah, the child colors the stone house and draws himself and his family inside the doorway. Then during the 'avodah, the child dips a vegetable with small leaves (such as parsley) into HaSeh's "blood," and paints it onto the doorframe.

Passover Teaching-Picture Craft

Complete instructions, templates, and more available online

http://passover.perfect-word.org

WHY SO "EXTREME?"

In my children's lives, an understanding of the events of Passover has been a key factor that led directly to their understanding of Yeshua's atoning work on their behalf. As they heard about the first-born sons of Israel being saved from death by the lamb's blood that was placed on the doorposts of their homes, their eyes were opened to see how they too could be saved by the blood of the Lamb of God, *Yeshua!* Tears flowed from their eyes as they committed themselves to Messiah.

And yet, as the years passed, the original impact of that moment began to fade in their minds. Though they understood that blood had been shed for them, it became an abstract concept that no longer evoked a response. I looked for activities or crafts to help cement the reality of Passover in their hearts and minds, but seder plate replicas and fluffy lambs made from hand tracings were all I could find. Everything was cute and sanitized, with all reality of blood and death removed from the picture. To me, these things are crucial for a true understanding of the price that has been paid for our deliverance.

This finally led me to create a craft of our own—one that would graphically depict the Passover sacrifice, if only on a small scale. The first time I attempted to make this little lamb, I was amazed by how easy it was to construct a basic replica of a lamb with just a few ordinary materials. But when I cut the lamb open, and saw the "blood" spilling from its body, I realized that the potential emotional response was *far* from ordinary—and it wouldn't be limited to children! Having since used this craft on several Passovers, I can attest that it will have a deep impact on both young and old, as our senses are reminded of the costly, bloody sacrifice that has been made forever on our behalf!

Suggestions for the Facilitator

See the *Behold the Lamb Preparation Guide* (available separately) for the fullest 'Avodah experience.

BEFORE YOU BEGIN...

- You will need the following foods:

    ❧ *Matzah (Unleavened Bread)*

    ❧ *Maror (Bitter Herbs; trad., horseradish)*

    ❧ *Fruit of the Vine (Grape Juice or Wine)*

- Familiarize yourself with the entire Haggadah in advance, so that you can progress through the 'Avodah without any awkwardness or distractions.

- Designate the additional readers as specified in the 'Avodah. The readers do not need to be seated consecutively; in fact, it is more dramatic when they are not.

- Plan to prompt the household with "Together..." for the "All" sections when needed, especially in the first half of the Haggadah. In later sections, the rhythm of the reading will naturally prompt the household to respond.

AFTER EVERYONE HAS GATHERED FOR THE 'AVODAH...

- Give the following instructions to the whole household:

    ❧ *All readers (including the Facilitator) should endeavor to read deliberately and with feeling. Don't rush!*

    ❧ *Speak—rather than sing—the traditional b'rachot (blessings). This helps to preserve the tone of the 'Avodah.*

    ❧ *When prompted to drink, do not empty your cup unless it is specified to do so—you will be instructed when to empty and refill your cup.*

- In response to the concluding "Amen," all are encouraged to:

    ❧ *Break forth in praise to God!*

    ❧ *Don't hold back!*

    ❧ *Celebrate the salvation of the LORD!*

Let us keep the Feast!

The night of Passover is just the beginning. Enter into the fullness of the Week of Matzah and beyond with the help of the **Messianic Mo'adiym Devotional**. Join Kevin Geoffrey as he offers insightful and uplifting devotional writings, designed specifically to be read during the annual appointed times as found in Leviticus 23 (one devotional for each day of every feast, including all 49 days of the Omer). *Available from Perfect Word.*

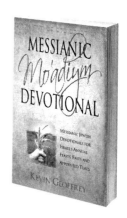

http://resources.perfect-word.org

Other books by Kevin Geoffrey

Deny Yourself: The Atoning Command of Yom Kippur

Giving ADONAI His Due: Praise and Worship (forthcoming)

Messianic Daily Devotional

Messianic Torah Devotional

The Messianic Life: Being a Disciple of Messiah

The Messianic Life: Bearing the Fruit of the Spirit (forthcoming)

A Messianic Jewish Equipping Ministry

CALLING THE BODY OF MESSIAH TO MATURITY
BY TEACHING THE SIMPLE APPLICATION OF SCRIPTURE
FOR A RADICALLY CHANGED LIFE IN YESHUA

www.PerfectWordMinistries.org

CPSIA information can be obtained at www.ICGtesting.com
Printed in the USA
BVOW030615240212

283723BV00005B/2/P